DAY

First published in 2006 by
Dedalus Press
13 Moyclare Road
Baldoyle
Dublin 13
Ireland

www.dedaluspress.com

ISBN 1 904556 52 3

Dedalus Press titles are represented and distributed in the USA and Canada by Dufour Editions Ltd., PO Box 7, Chester Springs, Pennsylvania 19425, and in the UK by Central Books, 99 Wallis Road, London E9 5LN.

Front cover image © iStockphoto.com
Design by Pat Boran

Printed and bound in the UK by Lightning Source, 6 Precedent Drive, Rooksley, Milton Keynes MK13 8PR, UK.

The Dedalus Press receives financial assistance from An Chomhairle Ealaíon / The Arts Council, Ireland

the arts council an chomhairle ealaíon

DAY

Amir Or

Translated from the Hebrew
by Fiona Sampson and the author

Published in Hebrew
by Tag / Hakibbutz Hameuchad, Israel 1999

Dedalus

For my mother and father

Mountain within mountain, bundle within bundle,
Piled-up sky covered the round of the seashore.
Beyond the line of kohl on the edge of the silver-leaf
Two masts sailed in the horizon that became light.

NOTE

'Day', the title sequence of this book, is the second part of a trilogy. *Poem*, the first book in the series, was published by Dedalus in 2004. The final section, *Night Scroll*, was published in Hebrew in 1999. The poems of the second section, *Day*, published here, take their cue from the Jewish Book of Prayers; and are preceded here by a selection of recent poems addressing related themes.

Day was first published in Hebrew by Hakibbutz Hameuchad and Tag, Tel-Aviv 1999.

We are grateful to the Board and Trustees of the Heinrich Böll Cottage, Achill Island, for a Fellowship, and to Bi-Arts / British Council for a research grant which enabled us to complete the translation of this book.

Amir Or & Fiona Sampson

Note on the translation:

Of the poems collected here, "Face" and "Song" were translated by Helena Berg.

Contents

Loot

Language Says

Language says: before language
stands a language. Language is traces
stained by over there.
Language says: listen now.
You listen: here was
            echo.

Take silence and try to be silent.
Take the words and try to speak:
beyond language, language is a wound
from which the world flows and flows.
Language says: is, is not, is,
is not. Language says: I.
Language says: come on, let's speak you,
let's handle you; come on, say
you've said –

Here

Here is my testimony:
about fifty, father to a six-year-old (you don't see that),
making words into poetry, loved, hated (don't see that), actually
a kind of wild creature, here:
soul cuts, rebellion, lips
too sensitive, all eyes
(as you see) and actually
what a mirror betrays is no deeper than what it doesn't,
what a mirror mirrors – is a two-dimensional Being-card,
framing the appearance of the Wanted. One portrait
glancing into a moment from the crowd of the soul;
and the soul?
What can I show you about it
which you don't already know?
Here's the wheat-stalk which grew out of nothingness,
here the knife
that cut it from the One.

Sunset

In this vulnerable, resting, light
the eye is thickened with shadow, deepened by absence.
Things hang in space, ground down by being seen, transparent –
and the mode they exist in now
is their mode of fading away.

The creating eye has weakened;
and the world that streamed – is almost already all sea;
whoever's in front of me, behind me, at my side –
is me, but isn't here.
And it's already late. And the day's over.
And we were left here, alone.

On the banks of the world
there we sat down, imploring our souls -
There we weep, eyeless,
when our gaze sinks into the great sea
and we suddenly remember
who we have been.

Succession

Appu, the first wise man, the half-human, was squatting, sticking out his lips, in front of the ears of barley which had grown from seeds fallen from his palm. For a moment he picked his nose thoughtfully; then stuck his finger in the wet soil, placed a seed in the hole and invented agriculture. That's how, say the ancient texts, Appu lay with the earth. In one syllogism, Appu saved man from the darkness of the eternal present and gave him past and future; with one syllogism he taught people to desire what's absent. This is how Appu entered the cave of death and discovered in it – culture. Therefore the proverb says, *All of our science put together is no more than a nit on Appu's skull.*

Hashi, the sixth wise man, stole barleycorn, stole the virginity of the earth priestess and stole fire from the heart of the flint mountain. He ground the flints together; he kneaded the priestess; he baked the earth. This is how Hashi invented bread. In one hour, say the ancient texts, Hashi stole poverty from the rich and foolishness from the wise. Therefore the proverb says, *Is Hashi here? – Mind your pockets! All of our wealth put together can't cure Hashi's poverty.*

Goma the Blind, the eleventh wise man, was the first to discover language. He slapped his belly, which made a dull sound, but in vain. *Bread!* yelled Goma until people learnt the secret of sign and signified. That's how, say the ancient texts, Goma pointed without a finger and saw without eyes. In one word Goma saved man from time and place and made the will grow wings. Therefore the proverb says, *All of our texts put together are as the eyes of Goma.*

Nano, the one-hundred-and-eighth wise man, looked around and saw nothing. He listened and heard nothing. He touched and felt nothing. With Nano, say the ancient texts, redemption came to the world.

Song

In the journey that doesn't end
everything and nothing are like waves.
arriving not-arriving –
and where am I?
I have no mouth nor face,
only a longing and a desert.

Give me an eye to expel
the mind into the fire;–
who I was I don't remember.
I have no tomorrow, only now,
only you, like a star I won't stop calling out for.
And I pass like a shadow
until you rise in the east
into a world of grey shadows;
until I'm thawed like the frost
and burnt in the light
and I can return to you, saying
that I'm already here.

Give me an eye to revive
a memory that hasn't been erased
from the soul that crossed
the whole desert with you,
from the water to the fire;
who I was I don't remember.
Wandering on a camel
the moon is my witness;
if it fall and die
I will bury my face
between sand and sand.

Give me an eye to expel
the mind into the fire,
and in the midst of what there is
let me dance empty as a whirlwind
until we fall here like shadows.

Let thirst drink from the well
for it will remain
like a burning memory
chiming after us
that the herd's nearing
and evening's falling again,
like a baby to a breast,
as everything turns to one,
as night wraps up
the tent and the heart again.
And then I too return –
a sound that has no beginning,
a song without end, wordless:
who were you all? I don't remember,
only a longing and a desert.
I have no tomorrow, only now,
no grave, only a star,
and from that place like hunger
I come to the heart that doesn't end
and I break here:
everything and nothing are like waves
arriving not-arriving;
if I have no *I* then who's inside?
Only a longing and a desert.

Translated by Helena Berg

The Temptation

In the deserted orange grove -
I was playing hide and seek alone
when on the high grass round me
presence fell.
The air was clear, the earth clear:
what could be seen was transparent on the eye
like a movie on a screen.

This was the temptation:
to rub the I against the you,
our thought against its images.
To feel.

We were there before, you remember,
without mother or father, without navel,
marked only by the first cut.
Free of weight, measurement, destruction
we wandered inside each other, dreamt worlds,
lived.
But the stakes were too low,
the risk – only a game.
Desire was action,
instantly complete.
And that's the way, you remember,
we got here too:
by a single desire,
by a glance.

And now we're here, in the viscous air,
rubbing this in, with effort –
every single sensation, every meeting.
Our suns rise and set,
our worlds get old,
but here:
suddenly we find
a new wrinkle in our soul,

and *this* – is for real. It's real. Finally
we can lose, destroy,
finally we are alive.
For a moment
we can even die.

Orphica

Tell me how to fight you.
- I'm holding your head. Night rises from the grass.
Tell me how to fight you.
- I'm stepping towards another realm. I have no mouth.
Tell me how to fight you.
- I'm swimming around my heart like a shark.
Now I see you. You don't exist.

- Tell me how to fight you.
I'm holding your head. Night rises from the grass.
- Tell me how to fight you.
I have a mouth. I place chopsticks on your face.
- Tell me how to fight you.
I sit on your heart like a cat. Far from the water.
- Tell me how to fight you.
Now I see you. I'm hungry.

El Amor Brujo

How to say this? You're too close to bear,
you are fruit bursting in the heart,
you are the name the dumb mouth bears
like sea in the earth's palm.
I touch, and envy my touching hand;
touching, I yearn to touch.

Terror of this motionless moment:
you are here inside here inside here.
Here the soul-fire burns, burns.
The heart unconsumed.

Old Song

Even the lightest separation has sorrow in it.
What we saw and were has passed,
fallen from our eyes and gone
piling one more autumn on our chests.

Even the lightest separation has sorrow in it
but when lovers go their own way
the heart burns unconsumed, uprooted but not rootless,
too heavy to bear.

Even if we shared the shadow of a tree on the road,
these lives of ours have passed like shadows;
or if we shared happiness in a view of sunset
our sun has set with it
                                        into a dark sea.

Twilight envelops all, the wind stops breathing;
but, beyond darkening light,
when they've circled their own sky, our eyes
will open again under lids of fog:

spirit's still blowing through the forest,
the shadow's still in the foliage,
and in the sunset that doesn't end
we'll separate for an infinity of love.

Shift

After some time the death-bird
started to cut through the murmurs of night.
On a blue coffin

sparrows were gathering straw-stalks and gleanings for a wreath.
Keening women, whose breath was getting short,
burst into their marvellous lamentation:
Even he who's free of everything
isn't free from being himself.

Foreigner

He wakes on scorching sand between wall and square.
In front of him the convoy halts, as in front of a forgotten memory:

is he just a road-marking, is he a signpost or a record,
was he left here at the fork in the road

for a moment or for ever? The body that stiffened didn't die:
look, he's not alone. Figures without shadows, casting no reflections,

carry him to be burnt
on a pile of fire-wood, dung and libations of oil,

under a heap of flowers. Is this a man or a fish?
Will he live or go, with his pallbearers, through

the gate that turns on the face of the turning abyss
on the unseen axis between rift and spring?

His hands, legs and neck are fixed in position,
in this one step with which he walked out beyond sight

and vanished into his shadow. His gills froze in a last breath,
his shadow remained behind him, yellow,

thrown down like a monk's habit, emptied-out,
to be trodden on by any passer-by along the rutted path

which runs between huts and peddlers' stalls; shadow, figure, costume
were scorched like a fiery image in the reflection

he left here: in a lover's eyes; looking out from a mirror-world on the house wall;
and in puddle-creatures flickering between rain and light.

Now he wakes, a disembodied figure carried like loot
in the hands of the eternal gravediggers. The funeral paces

inside the slow silence as if in a thick, congealing liquid;
the wailing women aren't seen, but their voices rise in lament: *Ya-hoi! Ya-hoi! Ya-hoi!*

The congregation is submerged, not fully cut out of the dark,
dragging after the pallbearers like a long wake of shadow, or foam

following a crab on-shore. Waking, he places his feet
on ground he didn't reckon with and hasn't remembered this time either; tries a movement

like a calf standing up for the first time on four feet to be licked by his mother's tongue.
Already the body-bearers recoil, even though movement's not visible

to the casual eye, but crawls inside his limbs like a branch growing.
He's been abandoned on sand, in a square, in front of a wall,

and while an age passes he finally stands; his shadow grows up the wall,
opens wide onto the square, he pulls the limbs of absence down towards him,

stretches out his hands to everything behind. Now, when he remembers,
he hesitates to touch what brought him here, the greatness which fell from him

with a single thought. Slowly he loosens himself
from the death-spasm; slowly he looks towards the reflection and shadow

he left behind: a wife and two daughters, a boy of five,
and an old mother who's still standing, like an echo that came back to its voice,

on the river bank where the ashes were scattered,
where Narcissus drowned.

Face

My head is a cloud on the face of the lake;
                                        the wind
                                        is peaceful.
Mountains and mountain shadows,
spots of grey and light,
travel over the mirror of water.
Spots of, shadows of, faces,
a long
            long procession.
Faces that have been
                                    will always be
here within here within here:
on the shore of an eye the dead gather
                                       to bathe
                                       to rise
                                       and be.

My face on the face of a lake,
ripples on the face of ripples:
Troy, Jerusalem, Alexandria, Rome
rise and fall
                                    fall and rise.
Smoke still rises from city walls,
swords still glitter at dusk,
I rise and fall, fall and rise.
Faces that will be always have been;
grey spots in the mirror of water.

Ohrid Lake, Macedonia, 2003

Translated by Helena Berg

Art

This was the eighth day of creation:
clouds absorbed burning brush-strokes
across the bluish-grey width of the sky.

Our souls struggled towards the fire
like beautiful insects
but the plane – was all forwards, drawing out its line.
Indifferent to the heavenly cataclysm
it passed far above.

At dawn under lampshades of clouds
the being-artist dipped his brush in thin light
and peaceful autumn was silently drawn into the tops of the plane trees,
gradually matching them with patches of roof
among waterfalls of Russian vine.

The air's clean of thoughts;
what can be seen – nameless, packed with dreams.
Between patches of wandering worlds, the world's
slowly rising
here and there, in my eyes.

Day

SHAHARIT

Morning Service

"My God, this soul, from thee derived, is, as thou gav'st it, pure;
By Thee created, formed, inbreathed, through Thee shall endure:
Till come the hour when thou shalt please to take my soul to Thee,
Returning it in heavenly grace in dim futurity."

"Blessed art thou, the Eternal, our God, King of the universe, who removeth sleep from mine eyes and slumber from my eyelids.
May it be thy will, O Eternal, our God and the god of our fathers, to guide our steps within the Law, and cause us to cleave unto thy commandments. Suffer us not to enter upon a course of sin, transgression, and iniquity, or fall into temptation and disgrace."

I

It's here, falling and expanding in nothingness, without prior notice
of the birth of a universe from this point of light: an eye appears,
half opens, shuts and opens
to see what there is to see; from an eye without an *I*, from outer light,
stains are already settling slowly on the face of the sun: a window frame,
its paint peeled into pieces of yes and no; through it –
ivy leaves dense with shadows, spotted with brightness;
not loosening their grip over the wall opposite they crawl onward from it
into the empty vessel that's already washed clean with blinding light,
into line with the eye that examines is and is-not; one more minute
and the last of the half-light will be finished in the memory-sky and the whole room
fill up with words:
bed-sheet, clock and, just here, hair sticking out from the blanket –
and it's not mine. And no, I don't want this. It's all yet another dream,
familiar like the others, but for some reason its images
are very resistant, and it's not enough to want them for them to materialize
as some kind of world.
After the light –
flesh: a wave of heavy opacity surrounds your will which is still intangible,
inanimate, not keen to carry the burden, to be a body again, to go out
from nothing to *there.* What can I do?
Hello my soul,
who'll give thanks for your safe return, *hup!,* into this clay
which immediately turns into an "I", as in any dream? And the *I* behind it all
that's all eyes – also returns, doesn't return, *here*
from its myriad lives, like Sinbad or Marco Polo; and already begins
to expand in the flesh, to wear a dull forgotten will
and close eye after eye – all of them – with a throat-less sigh:
except these two that look straight ahead
into the viscous medium. And already, while you're still outside these movements
you go out to conquer time and place for yourself: blanket aside,
the torso rolls half a turn on the elbow then spreads a pair of legs
to place the *I* into space itself; now
where are the slip-ons? The biped refuses, but nevertheless
the whole bundle makes its way between the walls to the door,
to find itself among white tiles, a sink, a mirror and water

in what, in a combined effort of palate, tongue,
lips and throat, is called "I'm going to wash".
Giving in to lighting effects and what appears below them
I look at the face of a portrait floating up in front of me onto a bright surface:
its features are a bit unstitched, its eyes are bleary, but see:
we haven't worn anything yet.
That's it. Get up
and get dressed right away: name, surname, profession, age, (bachelor?
married? divorced?) a shave, cologne, a brush of the teeth,
now a comb of the hair, trousers (the black
or the blue?), where are the shoes, the shirt? (maybe
need a jacket?) – a little green angel slaps you on your mouth
and you already forgot what you remembered, where you came from and where you're going;
conquer the world of a cup of coffee, and later – let's see. Fear reveals itself
as the hidden note in a ring-tone that's not fit
even for an Order of birds of prey. What d'you want from me?
What did I do? What haven't I given? Oh Gorgon,
cast your gaze upon me now, before I get used to moving,
before the day populates itself with its thousands of questions
that dance on the heads of pins
which pin up and close my openings over me – while I'm still alive;
teach me the secret of the mirror
and the peaceful silence of the wisdom of stone
in the face of the day's swarms of questions to which the single answer is:
here-I-am.

Newspaper, cigarette, more coffee, a window halved
between light and shadow; beyond it – the promised land,
clara et distincta, in which they're already emptying the dustbins
and sweeping up the dust with which the demons of entropy covered it all night.
"Newspaper", "table", "sugar caddy", a ceiling,
a floor and a door, a wall, a corner, another wall and another, a crack –
like a reminder note stuck to every single thing –
again teaching a routine going-through-the-motions
that contains nothing of the glory of their creation
but rather a call to order, which, through the power of a ramshackle miracle,
has enough in it to get them to share time and place
to the point of somewhat insecure dominion over a room's kingdom.
I go to the toilet and there study anew

who feeds and who's food; then let go of all this, surrender
before the goddess of Change, who digests the day
without passing judgment. Now I pass through myself, as she does;
I stop saying "I", and right away I am. Now
all this no longer matters, only: that I'll be
whatever will be.
Oh goddess of changeable forms, give me the strength to let go
and not *be* so much; to turn through all the faces
of this day; let me not freeze outside my heart,
not walk crooked through fear of the day's metamorphoses, not march in formation
with the rest of the faces that have already been,
and not wander being-not-being through invisible corridors
past the day's scenery; so I won't be ashamed to say:
"Here I am, talk to me in many voices,
from all of the *here*, from myself".

II

Another little angel passes by, all black and gold stripes, his wings
are transparent as light and his humming is like honey: hey, listen,
benevolence has run out. I zip my trousers, wash and dry my hand.
I hear the knocking of beak-on-a-window,
and myself look at the door, waiting for someone
to say from the other side, "Come in!". If birds
are already asking to live here in the apartment then surely, I think,
the trees outside have been cut down. Such things
can't really be verified, unlike the news
that the Number 5 bus was blown up, torn apart, chopped up
with all its chattering content even before I woke up. I'm not
prepared to be me in such conditions,
and like a plastic ashtray under a burning cigarette butt
just hurry to be covered by thought burns:
it's not today, it already happened half a year ago; your time –
passed. Stop! Come back! This bird
may be hungry for bread or company,
perhaps it fell captive to the magic of the knocking sound
and just kisses its reflection, which kisses it back in the window
in the pendulum double-swing of a "good-morning".
Then, from the beginning again, inhale another portion of morning
into your body which rests here, in one piece;
that cuddles itself as if in unending bosom –
and let's find out: were *you* on the bus?
No no: you only rang half an hour ago to say
that everything's all right, and we'll meet as planned in Café Gitane at four.
OK, I say; I let go of the receiver
and practice: "you" –
You glance calmly at me from the scatter of things seen
that recovers the reflection of your face
from all the *here* that was previously only "outside". Look,
I say, and fall silent, puzzled,
facing a new leaf that wasn't there yesterday evening,
that's folded a bit, glistening in its placenta, discrete,
busy with growing. Look, I say,
I don't want to remember you beyond your face,

but only see:
    ivy going up the wall opposite, a sparrow
knocking on the window, a newspaper, a table, a sugar jar –
    me, you, a new universe
that's waking up in the next room from apertures of eyes
    below black hair that sticks out from the blanket, and after it
again, of course, you:
    a little Japanese nose, a sweet mouth, a patch of neck,
breasts that sprout now, and happiness that rolls
  and already floods the galaxy: hello stars,
moon, sun, hello you –
    good morning –

III

Now I slowly open the outer door:
this happiness, how come?
One step over the threshold imposes further submission,
to a domain whose measure's the size of a grave
in the world which is yours and yet not yours;
the threshold is a secret, a call beyond
another Veil to where "be that you are"
is neither cheap nor winged –
in front of what stands here, outside fear and courage,
solid as a god of Stone with its face not yet carved
and the one who won't see it is "alive" only in name.
Outside, the day waits for outward action
cut, clear and sculpted, out of matter and light.
The goddess of Change reigns here without hurry
and already our will doesn't shape dream and shadow.
The matter of things, that returns to a distinct kingdom
sinking into itself again, into the weight of its being,
will be marker-stone and dwelling zone for us today,
a touchstone and whetstone for our disobedient spirit,
Promethean fetters on the rebelliousness of memory
that hasn't yet been sufficiently initiated
into the secret orders of sacrifices and the benevolence of yoke.

MUSAF

Additional Service

"He sustaineth the living in mercy and reanimateth the dead in abundant compassion, supporteth the fallen, and healeth the sick, releaseth those that are bound, and establisheth his faithfulness unto those who sleep in the dust."

"We will render thanks unto thee , and declare thy praise, because of our lives that are entrusted to thy hand, and our souls that are confided unto thee; because also of thy miracles that are daily shown unto us, thy wonders and thy acts of beneficence that are all times, at even, morn and noonday."

"Thou rememberest what hath been done from eternity, and passest in review all creatures of the remotest past... For the remembrance of all deeds cometh before thee, and thou scrutinizest the acts of all."

Like its predecessors, this day will be words
that, right here, one after the other
fall from it onto the sand and, further,
into the silence between the page
and its turning. It will be read from the beginning
without visible beginning,
with blind fingers, like a kind of a prayer for speechlessness
while we're here creating limbs for it.
And, just as from any other place, we'll start walking in the world:
gods reborn, we will emerge and be,
come as messengers equipped with instruments of sight,
taste, sound and smell. We will investigate: searching,
recording everything, movement by movement, to inspect
how it comes out of itself to us: call "Here it is" and it already is,
call "Land!" and your feet are already among stripes of shadow and light
that float in wet greenness, touching the skin
we wore especially for this journey from word to day.
Say "it's over there" and already the path turns
up-hill between the rocks on the slope; say "freedom"
and already above the fortress walls – smoke and cries of the wounded;
and until morning we'll continue saying "Out there the darkness burns",
and until dawn we'll say "Swing up the sun!"
and as the day ends we'll look back with pleasure or horror,
say "History", and gather what's seen
into a museum of memories that will be preserved from now on.

Only the silent and the mute, the delicate of blanket
and turners from side to side in perfect movements
won't be remembered or enumerated, except in accidental syllables:
day roamers and night rovers, village and city fools,
thirteenth-century *nargileh* champions,
expert whistlers, matchless flower-smellers,
masters of limitless gazing,
seers whom nobody sees, dream wanderers,
double agents of another reality
whom only poets are likely to praise –
but other speakers, whose words are well considered, name them:
face-parasites, the faceless, and face-multipliers –
should the day be given to them we'd still
be dwelling in caves and rock-clefts,

drumming on our thighs with rhythmic groans,
with neither destruction nor structure, without the strength
to become what we are not, without books, without histories,
without glory or disgrace, without a word
that's clear, challenging, decisive.
But this too is written in sand, even if with a sure hand;
and not this silence, but that meaningless babble,
is the jabbering baby-talk of humanity-in-potential;
the endless chanting of a frightened mantra
whose only virtue is games for bread and anaesthesia of the heart,
which isn't searching any mystery from morning to evening;
it has no modesty in it, but rather
refuses the grace of will – "Be that which you are".
On the other hand, because of too much fluency,
we've forgotten the blessings of those rich in nothingness
who speak clearly the untrodden path, the unwaved wing:
night-murmurs, landscapes of dreams that flow into the day,
the thundering of silence whose commandment
cuts through this journey with a forgotten memory:
where we came from, where to, and for what and why.
Therefore, you pearl-divers whose breath has been stopped up
by the terror of endless deeps,
dreamers of the infinite driven mad by the splendour of their vision,
sand readers, void-thinkers whose vision is too terrible for words –
speak silence to me with your whole voice
so I don't hear the choir of echoes:
"Whoever goes up will live, whoever goes down will die,
and whoever's frozen in blood-terror is neither alive nor dead".

Here! We've spoken the day. Here! The silent ones have been silent
and the speakers have spoken. In a little while we'll be called away,
in a little while time will return to its beginning;
all day long, night sits on our shoulder
whispering in our ear, "Listen, this too will pass".
Say "Here!" and here I am; be silent – and I haven't been;
before an endless hush falls;
the TV's still on, the clock's struck, and the corpse
cooling in watching position, in front of pistachios and beer,
a TV Guide in its lap,
is finally, with generous restraint, being peaceful:

"Morning and evening
are all one to me; it's all one to me what you say
and what I told my soul when she said 'good bye'. Now
I'll go back to my place, you – to yours".
But nothing will hush whatever we haven't been,
today, now, in the moment of action. For in a short while
we'll return to another beginning, no different from this one,
and what we haven't seen and heard,
what we haven't tasted and touched like a miracle,
will stalk our footprints – to get said, to exist,
to be carved in sand in one of the eternities,
to be gathered from our faces like a heavy crop:
a provision for the beyond, which already opens in front of us
like a hall of mirrors.

MINCHA

Offering

(Afternoon Service)

"Happy they who dwell in thy house, they shall be ever praising thee, Selah! – Happy the people that is so circumstanced, happy the people whose God is the Eternal!"

"And one calleth unto another saying: Holy, Holy, Holy is the Eternal of hosts, the whole earth is replete with his glory. And they receive from one another the word and say: Holy is the highest heaven of heavens."

"Satisfy us with thy goodness, cause us to rejoice in thy salvation, purify our hearts to serve thee in truth."

I

The day is a sun, a moon, and a meal
    devouring itself, the day is the life of one man,
the deaths of others;
    birthdays and death-days, the face of running water,
rhyming moments of eternity on an abacus.
    Look outside and see how they take the dead out
from the now to yesterday; look at the body, whose slow ruin
    is the relief of breathing out,
the calming of a storm in a sea of four ells*.
    Look at the faces of people in the street: only their body
is really passing the violets and jasmine in the yard
    and seeing, in the lot opposite, sharp indentations on the out-stretched surfaces
of castor leaves among briers flowering in purple clusters;
    stumbling over paving stones; swallowing sun;
dispersing its own smells in the air round about;
    passing through the market-place of being, where there are no sellers or buyers,
like water in a mud gully
    storming with growth and decay – buzzing of flies
swarming in the reeds on a carcass that was yesterday's prey,
    smooth silvery fish backs,
kingfishers' and ospreys' lookouts above,
    washed-up earth, seeds and dry rushes – ;
the body left alone, nursing-suckling, giving-taking as it wishes:
    all surrendered to blessed corporeality
that bears an infinity of *yous*.
    But peoples' minds soar away from all this
to the head's heaven and clouds; and wander about there
    between images that have already been and those that will –
if only we choose them.
    Their spirit blows from here to there
and has ten thousand arguments and discussions: the umbrella that disappeared,
    a neighbours' dispute over roof-tarring charges, the salary raise falsely promised,
the grandson's bar-mitzvah, a memory of perfume from last night, two packets
    of cream cheese, a jar of instant coffee and, if there are any left, some rolls,
"I told him to be home before midnight", a haunting unidentified portrait,
    a homework equation with two unknown values,

hunting for toads in a puddle that's turned into a lake in an unknown land,
    witches gathering among the shadows of the room by the toy box;
Life and the life-like are gathering in the street,
    roaming back and forth inaudibly;
and the street isn't filled but is still all outdoor bodies,
    clear and innocent within the audible tumult.

II

We've already cleaned the blood from the altars we used to call
"arterial roads", "compulsory conscription" – and side altars:

"family", "state", "workplace"
and also "school", "old people's home", "loony bin".

All are bright with the gleam of afterwards; only the knives remain,
the ploughs, pans, pitchforks, the ladles, the coals

still hissing: we thank Thee for today's sacrifice,
the bread and knowledge, the labour, the roof-beam

we might have been only this morning – but the forester sized us otherwise
and by noon we were food for the devouring fire before Thee.

By the sinks an old woman sits and wipes, her name unknown
and her wages flesh. And we too

are sitting around her and wiping – knife after knife – as if
this were just a hobby. My tongue's already forked, I leave the kitchen

for the Temple courtyard: there among the booths of first fruits
a potter displays his pots, an athlete his pose, a baker

attests to his dough, poets to their poems, we read unasked
to every passerby. Near the bowls meant for money

an old woman sits and spins, her name unknown,
her wages words.

I return to the kitchen, lean over the flame, put a coal in my mouth
to repent over the day: here come its trees, its inhabitants, its cafes and flying saucers,

cavalry, elephants, parchments: we just spoke and they were.
Where would they be if not for today's sacrifice,

offered with a willing heart, though ignorant;
where would we be without vessels to carry away the plenty;

without words to say “we bore and grew rich”;
without giving, taking, honouring the abundance wherever it’s found?

I spit out the coal, and it falls on the bosom
of a third old woman who shadows me,

her name unknown,
her wages a face.

III

Wearer of faces, goddess of Change,
    queen of time and mutability
who is unseen by the eye of day
    except body after body;
you who weave together hunger and satiety,
    swell women's bellies
and midwife time out of time;
    you who slip away terrible
into the tombstones of our memory;
    from foot to head you are one:
even though in our mouths
    your names are one by one.
Goddess of transition, wearer of faces,
    to you we stretch out our necks again:
at first like a stork
    spreading her wings in autumn
when longings call her
    from endless embodiment;
afterwards like a wild man after prey
    putting his ear to the earth,
wide open to the pulse of the deer,
    to hearing their heart listen;
and finally, when the day's finished,
    like a beetle in the shadow of grass,
whose dream doesn't distinguish
    between swarm and stems.
Immortal one, mutable one,
    you whose future is ancient,
who renew the day that has passed:
    evanescent one, even if you become
innumerable in your changes,
    we see you one in your changing
and in transitoriness we find peace:
    to you we stretch out our necks again.

IV

Not far from the tumult of the street, from bee-hives of calculated action and the din of thought,
beyond the towers of the swarm, beyond banks of paving stones and the outflow of asphalt rivers,

exposed to the eye of day and tanning herself, is the animal nakedness of the human city;
wide open like a cesspit, a confluence of tears and sin, Tel-Aviv's out there

yet within, pleasuring herself in an ebb-and-flow game,
in the abandonment of sand and water, in the rite of bathing and in sun worship,

and her meaningless murmur makes us forget
every human sacrifice, every labour, every brave act and every prayer answered through action.

Opposite, in front of the kurkar* hills chiseled out by wind and water,
is a palace somebody built from moist sand and left there with all its inhabitants:

king and queen, horses and horsemen, prince, jester, a bony secret counsellor,
a gardener, a child's tutor, an inn's prostitutes and a crowd of peasant farmers

with the smell of horse dung and hay in their clothes, a grim barman slicing a sausage
along a counter over which a baker's apprentice, a laundrywoman and a wandering barber

lean in drunken togetherness, listening to the stories of a one-eyed saddler
(who, as he tells it, lost his other eye in the service of the king, in one of those battles

against the invaders who came in black ships with crook'd prows).
Wait just a moment more, for one or a few lifetimes, before you raise their gazes towards you

as if you're a ghost that has clothed itself with the powers of the sea;
just one more moment, and already, outside, waves beat against the city walls,

a child tramples down the palace roof, a garden, huts, the harbour.
One more moment and, weighed down by history, citadel and town will crumble into sand

and a cheerful wind will blow, ploughing words into the soft limestone of the seashore:
"This too will pass".

But even it is only the handmaid of an eternity that rules with a high hand;
which has no end or beginning, no moment that has truly passed with no return;

the hour glass pouring into itself again, as you do, only turns and turns time into time,
the is – which a moment ago was still called *past* or *future* – into is.

And why should we accept some invisible giant looking down on us
as we rush between moments, burdened with the day's chores?

We are measure, stature, time; and the events of the world that, seen through peepholes,
pass before us, also stay where they are on the eternal shore.

True, Mr. Line is of the opinion that in his place, which is the only one, no living being has dimension,
whereas Mr. Plane laughs with all his breadth at the arguments of Line, but in turn denies height.

And what these 'scholars' say, and their dispute which has divided nations and families:
is this not delineated on the level of the book?* I pick up a sea-shell and put it to my ear,

another one to the second, and it's no longer possible to know
how many sea-shells and ears there are. What I hear is –

ARVIT

Evening Service

“Blessed art thou, O Eternal, King of the universe, at whose behest the evening darkeneth, who in wisdom openeth the gates of heaven, and whose understanding vatieth the seasons and arrayeth the stars in their watches in the firmament according to his will. He createth day and night, causeth the light to vanish before the darkness and the darkness before the light.”

“Cause us to lie down, O Eternal! in peace, and cause us to rise up, O our King! unto life.”

I

By now day's turning towards its beginning; going down
to the brink of the abyss we came up from

to *be* again, carving out for ourselves
body, words, history,

and faithfully following day whichever way it turned –
along pavements, to offices, into detention cells,

by corridors and down tracks, taking the left-hand lane,
on zimmer frames, handcuffed, in a litter under a canopy:

a victorious army, *comme il faut*, with all its shields and lances,
rams, horses, elephants, captives and booty,

flags, images of gods, seers and priests,
pen-wielding scribes, peddlers and wheat merchants,

camp prostitutes, barbers and cuppers –
and here He is ahead, rising like a sun of glory,

all-leading, all-showing, dressed with splendour and glamour,
his glance testing hours, hearts, sweat and hope,

marching with the morning's first offerings
and the noon offering,

sure to visit his servants, to redeem by his mighty work
the I from the I and the you from the you.

But day is coming back to its beginning,
and we, whither shall we go?*

II

This I that is silent only when not bleeding,
that isn't face nor better half, that is only

a wound, a doubting finger that has been and is not
at the end of the Siamese stump we share;

this I that bleeds only what it drinks in,
that bears no fruit and no growth, yet all the same grows

a mighty trunk on the brink of depths that widen here between us
to a sea with its cliffs and prey; bitter and sweetly cuddled,

without shadow, without the breast, unconsoled, unassuaged;
the I which is outside the garden; the forbearing, the despised;

this I which is not me, which is not you –
what shall we do with it? – We shall not do.

III

Death and yet more death.
We have stood in the square hungry to be and, like mountain shadows,

covered the city with pictures of a waking sleep.
Was she there or wasn't she?

A stranger in my body, able and yet unable, I tried the air:
"How many more years will we walk these dead sands?"

The mountain is glimpsed like a vision or a mirage. Sands move on underfoot
like a memory with no beginning, and each place is every place.

Does the way go up or down? Are you here, behind my gaze?
Is my gaze there, ahead of me? Where have we come from?

Alone, the two of us have crossed vast marshes on the slowly melting faces of the drowned.
For years we've been immortal.

In the attic, in Amsterdam, we saw terrible sorrow in the window.
How much longer shall we walk between death and death, sand and sand?

A new past give us, a new death give us.
Give us this day the life of the day.

ERUV

Mixing Together

"By virtue of this 'Mixing' be it permitted unto us to bake, boil, and warm up, kindle lights and do on the Day of the Festival all that is needful for the Sabbath, we and all who dwell in this city."

I

When the sun turns its shoulder,
   let's drink, brothers, from the vine's secrets,
sprinkle the Bacchic libation on stone
   and raise an awestruck cry in case
the gods wait furious: for our coal-tongues, burning
   with endless praise, for a night of drinking
whose memory will multiply and outlast us all.
   Measure out the wine, double it with water
to make a true symposium
   where we can taste the calm pleasures
of fluency, apt conversation,
   eloquence, witty idioms
of manifold beauty we'll arrange by the book
   without breakage or mess, as befits men like us.
From now till our death we'll have only this cup
   to wash down the cry nature's lodged in us,
to protect us from the chaos of plenty
   no words can express, that the wise don't see,
and befits only savages;
   rough liquor of first-pressed grapes
tasting of the fear, pain and trembling
   of a beaten-down, persecuted soul rising up
with a roar of desire from his burning reflection:
   making a cave-echo sacrifice to those spirits
of scrubland and bog by which void becomes pregnant
   with stupid vice and the poison of wrong.
But our god is measure: from low towards high –
   between evil and good, praise and reproach,
laughter and cries – we won't be their prey.
   Tighten and loosen the wine's bridle,
break it like a colt that's not begged or bribed,
   doesn't soften or suffer, but gallops to the bit
with Honour and Desire, all three harnessed to lift skywards.
   And we'll rise, confident, neither hurried nor tired,
till we arrive open-eyed, and orbiting earth and sky
   see what is   and is not;

sure-handed, drive on till we see revealed
    the presiding stars of occult knowledge.
Let's make our way, let's rise together,
    let's refill our cup so sadness won't seize us;
let's strengthen our horses not with hay but grape-must,
    to keep circling the vine's secrets
till night turns its shoulder
    and we fall, sink like stone.

II

Let's drink, brothers, let's touch glasses!
   Daylight's already smouldering, flickering.
Drink, get drunk to fearlessness,
   to the point where we'll know unknowingness –
sitting together, speaking togetherness
   without selling, without barter;
for this fantasy heart, the opening gate is
   wild night and the wine which
already fills our cup before we've been –
   for pouring in libation and a shout of triumph.

Let's drink, brothers, let's touch glasses.
   Daylight's already smouldering, flickering;
and as day falls away let's let go
   of tomorrow's and yesterday's worry and shout.
"Who cares about sun!
   So what that we're full of juice, then wither!"
Ageless, we go astray with mulled wine.
   For mead's our instructor teaching moment by moment
that harm has no eyes and a chain – no arms
   when our throat speaks wine.

Let's drink, brothers, let's touch glasses,
   daylight's already smouldering, flickering
and night's light beckons, seducing us
   with a ray that falls from the moon onto
a child's face, a mirror, and a skeleton's mask.
   We'll add only one string of vanity
in their honour to our harp –
   for here's our share – the drink of gods,
our peace in darkness: a moment's eternity
   serves our thirsty soul as drinking trough.

Let's drink, brothers, let's touch glasses,
   daylight's already smouldering, flickering!
Drink, get more drunk, till we pass out –

yes with no, foe with friend,
with a light unsatiated heart –
to the festival that means nothing,
neither hope nor lack.
Garland for crown and cup in hand
we'll go out embraced to night,
an insatiable yes, and in the concealing darkness
utter the living word as gift:
Let's drink, brothers, let's touch glasses!
Night's light already beckons, seduces us.

KIDDUSH

Sanctification

"Blessed art thou, the Eternal, our God, King of the Universe, who created the fruit of the vine."

"Blessed art thou, the Eternal, our God, King of the Universe, who hath sanctified us with his commandments and found pleasure in us."

"Blessed art thou, the Eternal, our God, King of the Universe, who bringest forth bread from the earth."

"Blessed art thou O Eternal, our God, King of the universe, who created joy and gladness, bridegroom and bride, gladness and jubilation, exaltation and delight, love and paternity, peace and friendship."

I

Drink, heart, from the heart of the wine;
    empty a glass from is to is not.
Come, heart, say from where
    this painful arrow was fired into you;
who with bow-and-arrow craft
    chased you into trap and net
to capture you, chain you
    to my eyes like a slave.

Drink, heart, from the heart of the wine:
    empty a glass from is to is not
and lightly take turns in the dance of shackles.
    What dark longing's subdued you, wild thing,
so that head-lowered, chastened,
    you chase your own shadow?

Empty a glass of nothingness;
    drink, heart, turn into wine:
what the eye's lit upon
    in endless longing
will cover it like the water
    in a heart with no shore.

II

Let's love before nightfall, live, love! –
Give the whole day for one moment,
give and not miss it, die in a kiss
for a thousand eternities!

Come drunkenness, cover us both
with one blanket of forgetfulness;
a thousand kisses to you, and few coppers
to old Charon –

You who come out of formlessness, the turn of your neck
is so beautiful it hurts. Unveil your face!
I'm ripped-off skin, I'm flesh in your flesh,
you see me – and are gone.

III

The togetherness we are, which we remember even if we've forgotten it –
seed in the wind, cell to cell, one blood cycle,
a mouth on a breast, air roots, a cord of fog stretching from the navel –

The togetherness we are in that first knowing in a sudden encounter on the street,
in a gaze above and the heat of thigh below, limitless naked skin
within an unknown land, within the promised land, within that solace –

The togetherness we are at the bus stop, in neon-stricken offices,
carried on or carrying stretchers,
around the dummy in the circle-game, around the open grave, around the dinner table –

The togetherness we are, wordless, without skin, not pausing
in the rhythm of breath that becomes one in love or fear,
through the window opposite, through a yellowing photograph, through a goodbye letter –

The togetherness we are that has no unbruised spot at all, that has no consolation,
that is nothing but longing, mother's smell and father's, a hand stretched
and stretched, a hand put to the mouth, and hush –

The togetherness we are, wide open yet who dares look at it,
we circle round it like butterflies round a sun,
round the heat and light of a steady sacrificial fire –

The togetherness we are that every place is full of, whose limbs we are:
don't let's unveil its face, for if we do – we'll perish;
let us touch and yet not touch, see and not see, bow down before, fall silent.

NEI'LA

Concluding Prayer

(After Atonement)

"O Lord, open my lips, and my mouth shall declare thy praise! Remember us unto life, O King, who delightest in life! And inscribe us in the book of life for thine own sake, O ever-living God!"

"What are we? What is our kindness? What our help? What our strength and power? What shall we say in your presence, Eternal? Are not all heroes as naught before thee, and men of renown as though they have never been; the wise as though void of knowledge, and men of intelligence as though deprived of understanding? For the multitude of their deeds are mere emptiness, and the days of their lives a fleeting breath before thee."

I

A violet stripe encircles the sky and covers the greying blue on the eastern horizon:
a pink glow roofs and separates it, in the dusk,
from the rest of the blue above. Closer, but perhaps in the sky itself,
a pine tree's filling up with clods of dark foliage; within the hills and dales
of a green range the surface of its smooth trunk reveals itself only here and there,
incompletely rounded by the Artist of Being's hands. Right now, from the west
he's slowly pulling, down to my loins, a ball of fire that blazed all day
under his bellows, and finally, cooled, dives beneath edges of cloud
already blown with mist and light. And Nuth* is bending, her back turning pale,
from over there to over there; and her navel's a vast dome of dim bluish darkening light
whose crown is above mine; from her to me, into the dome of my head,
fullness falls in a beam towards which all of me grows: while I go on touching tree-life here
the tumult of people and cars stays far below us at my feet. Thoughts blow about,
down below in my tiny figure by the pine, too far away to be heard or understood.
A deep voice sinks inside me, within the resonant dome, and a high cool gust
enters and passes through me, air within air.
A swift eternity passes. A smell of rosemary: and a hand made to measure, my hand,
stretched out to touch it very, very closely. Together in slow motion in the remainder of the light,
all the you is crawling around, face within face, not keeping its distance.
The light's already thin, it fades, scattered and alien, dust glowing with tiny specks
which stray all round, afloat, while darkness collects among the tilth, lurks between it
and fills up the face of the stone floor with springs of shadow. Below,
dimness flows among small mounds and crevices down to canyon bottoms
filled with silt and earth. Leaning both my hands on the rocky wall I go down into it,
down the slope of the womb, in crevices carved in shadow; and from there further down;
glance beyond the curve of the cliff towards the sudden edge, into the grave,
at a depth that gapes under my gaze. Now I slowly lift my head to the remaining height;
a blotch of moss darkens above me, a rustle, a bird shrieks, and the whole pine
falls into my eyes.

II

The water is rolling you, rolling
    rolling you until you're smooth, smooth, smooth;
and still – while day turns away and the surfaces of things seen
    open, weary of bearing their borders and being filled with shadow –
I don't want to remember You,
    only to watch Your face and nothing beyond it. Yet, like an undeciphered revelation,
on this night a dark bird passes in front of the windscreen
    above an asphalt strip between two rows of eucalyptus;
emerges from shadow, takes on form for a moment in the car headlights
    and is again nothing but darkness; was or wasn't there.
The road twists further, at the range of a headlight in the dark,
    and this one memory is lit by a haunting light: what was that,
and why was it? It's hard to be sure about this sort of thing and we don't, for now,
    have a hold on that realm where the Goddess of Change reigns alone;
and maybe such a bird is an omen for something
    which is also in turn a word that took on form. Like that bird, the substance of things
is as though redeemed from weight, after serving us all day long as a border marker
    and a touchstone to keep us from falling into a continuing inertia,
from not being sufficiently present. But now – when daylight, in which we've been taught
    the order of sacrifices and the labour of quarrying, is finally removed from the world,
as at the end of an interrogation – heaven already stretches out its neck to us
    and in front of the red horizon what's seen is being unstitched. Our boiling blood
calms in the clouds; and slowly, like a cool mist, dream and shadow
    rise again in our bodies. It's almost time to let time subside
and place take off its dimensions; to dismantle the face
    we wore to face the dazzling brightness, the measure, the other,
and to let it go, let go – if only we can remember to.

    But we've forgotten: on and on, not letting go, we're in love
with the Luciferic light; and we notice, on the hill opposite, blue and yellow lights
    thrown like enigmatic script on the huge body of the dark
already herald another kind of unknowing: an ambulance siren
    goes up and down from the street, or maybe from the television,
climbing an in-your-head ladder up to the roof of the house, and from there –
    out to the sky:
a beam of fire pierces the smog,
    subsides slowly,

and is already returned to the city god's sheath.
Yet even here, nocturnal trees are not day-trees; shadows drop from them onto pavements, patios,
and onto the road that stretches towards the inevitable.
And if we're worthy, a longing like a messenger with a crossed-out letter in his hand,
emerging from the darkness into the living room, hands over to us
the instruments of nothingness, and proclaims out loud the howling of our heart:
"Where is the winged omen that hurried over the road in the dark?
When will the way take off into the darkness and lead us back home?"

Let's look, before we wipe the view from the windscreen again, and see this place
in which all times are present, all of whose faces record a response to being
and whose boundaries are only what they've always been:
bowl placed at the set time beside the kennel, then one or two wags of the tail
en route to an evening of snoozing in a corner of the apartment building guarded by hundred
watt bulbs:
while outside the wolves turn into man and spirit and howl, against the moon,
the prayer of change that descends slowly onto wastelands, shrubberies and fields,
and give thanks – for its blessing that we've repudiated for now as if it were some sort of ending.

But all the faces waking up in the rocks now, all the eyes floating
with yellowish radiance in the chilly valley, all the voices of night creatures which have
lost their forms and the whole
congregation of pale-browed mists returning to their kingdom, sweeping in victoriously –
just wait at the border of the light till it's turned off behind our eyelids,
till we agree to unload our by-now-heavy wakefulness and to let go, sink deeply, deeply
and far: bodies next to bodies, stretched out or coiled like foetuses,
wrapped in blankets or naked under a mosquito net, some embracing, some shuddering,
broken by dream, all finally unpacked onto mats and mattresses
while we're migrating to another realm and – lightly, like a flicker of light in rippling water,
through labyrinths of granite and dragonflies, through melons' aroma, the sound of bells
or corpses' stench,
growing gills, hair, hands, walking on thick carpets, flying, straying in unknown cities –
being flogged and tortured, oppressing and torturing, escaping an enraged mob at the last moment,
collapsing in the toilet, falling from a cliff, meeting an angel,
running through a gaping wheat field or leading an army in shining armour;
wearing landscapes, faces, time, without calculations or responsibilities
except the ones we've brought with us from today as provisions for tomorrow's road –

and that tomorrow with its yesterdays, like an onion being peeled,
spreading into its many, multiplying paths that will be walked over and over, with all their splendid décor,
the whole of which is reality. And beyond: more onions, universes that have been here
and others that aren't yet, worlds of our subjects, minute organisms of the hive of our flesh,
stars of particles whose awareness is shining universes of sound and eternity –
all in one point, open, limitless and timeless –
for the meeting of the soul faces all of which are Me.

III

We return to watch a sea
    that we've seen only from afar
from a slit opened through twilight, not from the shore.
    And in-between, when the room turns into water,
before we fall asleep from here and wake to over there,
    we're laid like foetuses in the belly of the ocean; touching the void
while further away from us the body shakes in its sudden fall
    the soul wakes itself up slowly to its world, and, in an ancient garden of flesh,
opens up its limbs to a history of movement in movement:
    the face of a dying Greek still proud of its restraint above a shuddering body,
seductive motion of a tavern-singer's hip, the gaitered legs of a horseman
    spurring his horse to a gallop along snowy shores
or the trembling of the reed pen in the palm of an old copyist.
    Faces that until now bent
over railings either side of the day
    and that just glanced repeatedly out of a borrowed existence
from a hallucinatory light at the margins of our eye,
    as if even before they existed
the day wherein they were born had perished.*
    We, rushing from the clear to the clarified,
forget even before we remember them;
    like the almost-touch on hip or back
of a passer-by's hem in the street.
    Yet in spite of that – now, before we put on faces like clothes,
when the *here* is thrown into the *there*
    and we're wandering, still naked, between domains
like déjà-vu spirits from another realm –
    we glance out of a hallucinatory light in the margin of their eye
or appear at will in the no-man's lands within gazes which aren't ours,
    between the *was* and the *wasn't* that still very much was,
to the right of this day where we've turned left,
    passing over on dry ground.*

TIKKUN

Correction

(Making Amends)

"O may it be acceptable in thy presence to make expiation for all our sins...

For the sin that we have committed in thy presence on compulsion or voluntarily;
And for the sin that we have committed in the utterance of our lips;
For the sin that we have committed in public and in private;
And for the sin that we have committed through unchaste indulgence;
For the sin that we have committed through lewd associations;
And for the sin that we have committed through violence; ...

Yet for all of them, O God of forgiveness, forgive us, pardon us, give us remission!"

A Correction

for the sin of being spoiled with words and mistaking the call of Love;
for turning away from myself like shadow from body, face from heart;
for the sin of 'What will they say?'; for self denial; for pride;
for the sin of having followed the spell of praise under the stage lights;
for my ear that has abandoned listening,
for the utterance of the mouth which I have spoken, yet my soul has not;
for sin I've committed against my own body with the rod and no kindness, beating my breast;
for calling Yours my own;
for having sinned before You by anxiety and vain fear,
for having fed the fire of doubt from the log of the tree of plenty;
for having been dilatory in growing;
for having shut my door and having neither heard nor seen nor let happiness enter me
when beholding Your being.

SHMA

Hear!

(Prayer On The Bed, Before Sleep)

"Hear, O Israel, the Eternal is our God; the Eternal is One!"

"Blessed art thou, O Eternal, our God, King of the universe, who causest the bands of sleep to fall upon my eyes! And illumine mine eyes lest I sleep the sleep of death, for thou art he who enlighteneth the apple of the eye."

"Thou in whose hand is the soul of every living creature, and the spirit of all human flesh. To thy hand do I command my spirit, thou redeemest me, O Eternal, God of truth."

Hear me now, even as I call unto You half-way through the night;
for my soul grows weak unless you nourish my spirit to sufficiency.
My heart is yearning but not afraid: let me walk here, half-way through the night.
Though I walk through the shadow of the valley,
like a baby remembering his conception I remember even if I have forgotten:
the faceless night gives wings to a memory of the One that has no other;
and an unconsoled longing falls with this hush on the whole people I've become. Now –
in a taken-apart love that won't ever be achieved,
whose redemption with each offspring is merely a distancing by one more generation –
look from the dark side of my pupils and see what sees in me:
jackals have already returned from rending their prey and owls have swallowed their gobbets,
the cities of men have melted into their own lamps, and the mountains' shadow
has spread out its slopes swarming with creatures of night.
Ships of mist have stopped collecting
dream travellers from stations of the upper air
and, absent, losing its face, everything sinks
to the bottom of itself and, laid down there
in the great night's rest, is gathered to its beginning
like a sort of a snake that has just finished swallowing its tail.
The darkness is deepening and there are no dreams in it. *Here* goes to its rest,
pulsating between being and non-being, inward and outward,
and within its wide spaces, under our eyes extinguished by their own lids,
our flesh flickers its worlds peacefully:
dew that dries easily under the sun's heat; flesh that perishes easily,
returning with night to the fields; nerve-endings
that have just been disconnected from high-voltage charges;
the heart that turns transparent like an unborn chameleon;
and limbs loosening from action, all dream, sinking in peaceful digestion,
like herds of antelope that came back from the pasture
to turn again into shadows. Thus I too
know without knowing, being pulled like a sperm in the ovary
to the eye of the great rest, to the mouth of a vortex that whirls around
what opens from there: countless paths for selves
through a sieve of spiral routes of is-was-will be.
A capillary of blood in the spreading body, I pulsate
in the beats of the whole soul, growing towards it, and spread
into the swarm of all the swarms of the *be – was* pulse
with a single aspiration. Like an opened code
my mind stretches out to touch inwards, touch the whole of the *I*-people,

its universes and the entirety of their creatures: this *I* body
whose myriad cells are the host of inner heaven, constellations and constellations
of interior stars with all their inhabitants and lives
flickering remote life forces in the distances made by amazement,
in one composite tone extending from beat to beat
and gathering itself again into an exhalation of life – to empty itself, to be just
a possibility of being, just a spark of a swollen-inside-itself universe.
And like a single molecule at the end of an amino acid,
or like a crystal taking shape with no knowledge of its body's appearance,
like the creatures of my spirit that are hidden from the eye –
so, I, too, am the tip of an apostrophe without dimension or duration
inside another universe beyond my comprehension, that I don't have the image of;
having a form I can only conceive of from this dimensionless existence.
I'm only the abundance passing through me and further, world
unto world, from possibility to its release, and again from existence
to its thirst to be. But time doesn't exist here:
hand on your mouth until our veiled faces are given back to us
to remove one mask for another one; until the hems of nothingness
are rolled up, a thin purple, from the lower rim of the dome of darkness,
and without advance notice a universe is born out of a speck of light:
an eye emerges, half opening beyond the earth's vault
to see what's there to see.

Notes on the Poems

P. 36: *Four ells.* In Hebrew tradition 4 ells is the measure of a human grave, the size of a human body.
P. 41: *Kurkar.* A very soft limestone that forms hills by the Mediterranean shore in Israel, Kurkar is easily carved and shaped, rounded and hollowed by the winds and moisture of the sea.
P. 42 *is this not delineated on the level of the book?* Literally 'on the book of Jashar' (Joshua 10, 13) which may mean in Hebrew 'the book of the plane' as well as 'the book of the righteous'.
P.44 *Whither shall we go.* In Gen. 37, 30, on seeing that Joseph is missing, Reuben says: "The child is not; and I, whither shall I go?"
P.60 *Nuth.* The Egyptian sky goddess was depicted as forming the dome of the sky by leaning over to touch Earth again.
P. 64 *the day wherein they were born had perished.* Job 3,3: "Let the day perish wherein I was born."
p. 64 *passing over on dry ground.* Joshua 3,17

Afterword by John F Deane

For Amir Or language is more than a method of communication between people by means of words; it is a power in itself. Language, its syntax, its grammar, its tendons, communicates by the pauses between words, by the juxtaposition of words, phrases and images, and by the stretches of silence between period and sentence-start. The language of a poem implicates both the reader and the writer; the implications for both are serious and worthy of examination in themselves. Out of this demanding and fruitful exchange, Or's poems achieve a new density and power, touching on springs in his and our being that are deeper than we may at first be aware of.

Here, then, is a poet whose every movement into language opens wounds in our sentimental and scared approaches to living. He is a poet who dares, in our time, to mention the 'soul'. He is a poet whose awareness of Old Testament poetry rings easily and true, like water echoing in the heart of a cove:

> On the banks of the world
> there we sat down, imploring our souls —
> There we weep, eyeless,
> when our gaze sinks into the great sea
> and we suddenly remember
> who we have been.

This is the metaphor of exile, deeply stirring both to a poet writing in Israel and to an audience from a shifting and shiftless continent like ours. Myths of all sorts are rich in our heartland and chime like memory, but it takes a conjunction of honest experience and linguistic heartiness to create the epiphany that will touch that depth. Again, here is a poet who cares about reaching so far, in spite of the demands of contemporary culture for superficial finesse and glitzy ease. Or's work asks more of the reader, he asks for this entering into the world of language the way the poet enters in; he demands the same sacrifice to truth the poet makes: and this is the "terrible angel" that a poet like Rilke speaks of; it is also the silent absorption in great things that Yeats saw in his "long-legged fly". The power of Or's myth-making, of his entering into the deep, can be quickly seen in the terrifying and beautiful poem, "Foreigner".

> He wakes on scorching sand between wall and square.
> In front of him the convoy halts, as in front of a forgotten memory:

is he just a road-marking, is he a signpost or a record,
was he left here at the fork in the road

for a moment or for ever?

This is the lyric poet entangled in the rough thickets of real living; it is also the epic poet capable of such a large foray into the territories of our nightmares that both he and we emerge again, shaken but conscious of the deeper honesties that make life worth while. And such a large foray is more in the keeping of this poet with his mythopoeic vision; such a large foray we have already witnessed in his earlier work "Poem" (Dedalus Press, 2004) and here in the longer piece that gives the book its title. In an earlier piece he can write:

Between patches of wandering worlds, the world's
slowly rising
here and there, in my eyes.

Like a growing awareness of the world in childhood through adolescence and into adulthood, the poem "Day" takes us on a journey/pilgrimage of understanding. To those of us versed in Christian terminology, Or's structuring here may be compared to the use of the canonical "hours" of the day, moving from Matins through to Compline. Here Shaharit, for example, is a prayer that may be recited from the rising of the morning star until one third of the day has passed; Abraham instituted the morning prayer service. So this prayer corresponds to the daily morning sacrifice offered in the Temple.

Such structuring of a poem or sequence is not uncommon, witness R.S.Thomas in his "Mass for Hard Times"; it is a meaningful and suggestive structure, carrying with it associations and relevancies that stand beyond the actual phrases of the poem. Amir Or does not simply let this structure look after itself, however; he uses it to examine words, relationships, the work of the soul in a universe shimmering between "is" and "not-is". The poem remains firmly in the world of reality: "bed-sheet, clock and, just here, hair sticking out from the blanket", the accurate details accurately relayed that bring us physically into the poem. The world of the everyday is darkened by a sense of fear: "the Number 5 bus was blown up, torn apart, chopped up with all its chattering content even before I woke up". Hence the greater importance of working out personal relationships, and how words go to develop such relationships. And if a sense of fear permeates, so does a sense of the richly prayerful past, the music of the Old Testament poetry with its pleas to the distantly hovering Deity, the relationship of suffering humanity to that Deity, and the sheer fragility of human living.

and here He is ahead, rising like a sun of glory,

all-leading, all-showing, dressed with splendour and glamour,
his glance testing hours, hearts, sweat and hope,
marching with the morning's first offerings
and the noon offering,

sure to visit his servants, to redeem by his mighty work
the I from the I and the you from the you.

Amir Or does not offer facile answers; he offers a poetry that is memorable, demanding, linguistically rich and accurate. He moves through a mesmeric range of line lengths, from the meditative longer line to the fast and furious shorter lines where breathing becomes difficult and the heart flutters in response. This is a poetry of note, a work to be taken seriously and spread around, a poet who bestrides several traditions with seeming ease, a special contribution to world poetry.

The translation, by Fiona Sampson, is immaculate. It is a commonplace to say that a good translation reads as if it were the original language; let me then offer that commonplace, for such is the case here. Not only does the English read as accurate English, but sound-patterns, internal chiming, the pace and pacing of the original, are caught so that the reader marvels at the lines; this is translation at its very best:

for calling Yours my own;
for having sinned before You by anxiety and vain fear,
for having fed the fire of doubt from the log of the tree of plenty;
for having been dilatory in growing;
for having shut my door and having neither heard nor seen nor let happiness enter me
when beholding Your being.

About the Poet

AMIR OR is a poet, translator, and editor. He has published seven books of poetry and volumes of his poetry available in English translation include *Miracle* (Poetry Ireland, Dublin 1998), *Language Says* (Poetry Miscellaneous Publications, Chattanooga, 2001) and *Poem* (Dedalus, Dublin 2004; Polish and Romanian editions, 2006). He has also published *Poetry is a Criminal Girl* (Arabic, Faradis, Paris 1995) and *Drowning, He Breaths Living Water* (Macedonian, The Peliades Series of Struga Poetry Festival, 2000) and his poems have been published in anthologies and poetry magazines in more than 25 languages. Or has participated in many international poetry festivals and conferences; and been a guest writer at several cultural institutions, among them the Literarische Colloquium Berlin, and Nihon University, Tokyo. For his poetry he has been awarded the Prime Minister's Prize, the Bernstein Prize and a Fulbright Award, as well as Fellowships at the University of Iowa, the Jewish-Hebrew Centre of the University of Oxford, Hawthornden Castle Scotland and the Heinrich Böll Cottage Achill Island, among others.

Or studied philosophy and comparative religion at the Hebrew University in Jerusalem, where he later lectured on Ancient Greek Religion. He has published articles on poetry, classic studies and religious studies, and has taught poetry and creative writing in Israel, the UK, and Japan.

Or has also published several books of translations into Hebrew, including *The Gospel of Thomas* (1992), *Limb-Loosening Desire - An Anthology of Erotic Greek Poetry* (1993), *Stories From The Mahabharata* (1998) and *To a Woman by Shuntaro Tanikawa* (2000, with Akiko Takahashi). For his translations of poetry from Ancient Greek he received the Honorary Prize of the Israeli Minister of Culture.

Since its foundation in 1990, Or has been Editor-in-Chief of Helicon: The Society for the Advancement of Poetry in Israel. He has initiated and developed Helicon Arabic-Hebrew Poetry School and is Editor of its journal and series of poetry books. He directs the Sha'ar International Poetry Festival and is national coordinator of the UN-sponsored "Poets for Peace".

About the Translator

FIONA SAMPSON has published twelve books, including four collections of poetry, philosophy of language and books on writing in health care. She has won many awards and been translated into fifteen languages; her books in translation include *The Self on the Page* (Hebrew, 2002), *Travel Diary* (Macedonian, 2003), *Folding the Real* (Romanian, 2004) and *The Distance Between Us* (Romanian, Macedonian, 2005). She is the Editor of *Poetry Review.*

Printed in the United Kingdom
by Lightning Source UK Ltd.
110055UKS00001B/49-192